Worthy TO Write

Worthy TO Write

BLANK PAGE TYING YOUR STOMACH IN KNOTS? 30 PRAYERS TO TACKLE THAT FEAR!

by the Pencildancers:
Diana Lesire Brandmeyer,
Angela Breidenbach, Liz Tolsma,
Jennifer Vander Klipp

Tandem Services Press
GRAND RAPIDS, MICHIGAN

Copyright

© 2017 by Diana Lesire Brandmeyer, Angela Breidenbach, Liz Tolsma, Jennifer Vander Klipp

Published by Tandem Services Press
Post Office Box 492
Belmont, Michigan 49306

www.Tandemservicesjvk.com

To the Lord Jesus Christ who makes the work of our hands something beautiful, to Him be the glory!

We, the authors of this book, want to speak joy and courage into you as a writer. We pray that as you journey through this book, you'll learn that you truly are Worthy to Write so that your joy will be full.

My heart is stirred by a noble theme as I recite my verses
for the king; my tongue is the pen of a skillful writer.
Psalm 45:1

Table of Contents

Does your stomach tie itself in knots thinking about showing others your work? Yet you know God has put this desire to write within you. The following prayers, written by seasoned writers who well know what it's like to feel unworthy, will fill your heart with courage, strength, and purpose.

Throughout the prayers, there will be blank spaces after each author's section to write your own response and pour out your heart to your Heavenly Father.

And as a bonus, have you read books by Diana Brandmeyer, Angela Breidenbach, Liz Tolsma, or Jennifer Vander Klipp? We've included some samples in the back by the authors of these prayers so you can get a taste of their writing as well.

Photo credit: Sara Lesire

Why, my soul, are you downcast? Why so disturbed within me? Put your hope in God, for I will yet praise him, my Savior and my God.
~Psalm 42:11 (NIV)

Heavenly Father,

Today my creativity is curdling like sour milk. Every plotline reeks of the wickedness of this world. How can my characters fight the evilness in the story? There are readers who will identify with the chaos and darkness of this storyworld and that makes me sad. Please draw the readers through my characters into peace where they will praise Your great name.

I look to you for hope to write your desires, to not fall into the darkness with these characters, and for those who will read this story.

Thank you for always being beside me, surrounding me with your love, and coaching me though the difficult parts of this writing life. I pray that you will find me worthy of this calling.

Amen

Do not gloat over me, my enemy! Though I have fallen, I will rise. Though I sit in darkness, the LORD *will be my light.*
~Micah 7:8 (NIV)

Heavenly Father,

Today my brain is filled with darkness. There is no glimmer of the words I need to write. The enemy is laughing because I want to put words into a story that will shine a light on your love, and I can't.

My fingers are leaden on the keyboard. Each word difficult to construct and type. The story itself is hidden from me.

You are my light, Father. Cast out the darkness, send the enemy from me. I praise you in this place of no words. I wait on your timing to shine your light and increase my excitement for writing the stories you are giving me.

I am forever thankful to call you Lord, Abba, giver of all that is good.

Amen

Photo credit: Sara Lesire
But Jesus often withdrew to lonely places and prayed.
~Luke 5:16 (NIV)

Heavenly Father,

Finding a quiet place seems impossible, and yet I am so lonely. No one in my family or friends understands the difficulties of writing. Everyone thinks it is a hobby, or that it's wonderful to hangout at home all day and play on the computer. They don't understand the pressure of creating a work from nothing more than an idea, a name, or a place while being surrounded with undone chores.

I'm so grateful you understand creativity. You thought up the entire universe and me. You knew the oceans would need coastlines. You knew I would need boundaries to keep me at my desk. You've taught me to say no to fun, but distracting, activities. You've used loneliness to draw me closer to you. You've rewarded me with writing friends who understand this life.

Thank you, Father, for always being with me. Thank you, for your Son so that I might know I'm not alone.

Amen

Photo credit: Sara Lesire
I am no longer worthy to be called your son; make me like one of your hired servants.
~Luke 15:19 (NIV)

Heavenly Father,

I'm flat on my face in front of you. I am a mere writer, how can I be your son or daughter? I'm fit to scrub your heavenly floors and nothing more. Can what I do bring you the glory and honor you deserve?

Show me that I am worth even of a small glance from your glorious face. I am not a psalmist like David. I am me. Yet David was a shepherd boy, and you loved him so much you changed his life. You made him a king, and you loved his writings. I, too, am a writer of small books. Am I as important to you as David?

My heart swells with love, and I rejoice at the honor of being one of your chosen. Let my words honor you. Let me work for you like a hired hand and be satisfied with the love you've given.

Amen

For we are God's handiwork, created in Christ Jesus to do good works, which God prepared in advance for us to do.
~Ephesians 2:10 (NIV)

Heavenly Father,

What a joy to read this verse today. I want to print it out and read it every morning when I sit at my keyboard to write. You did know me before I was born, and you have a plan for me. You created me to write for you, not always for others, but for you.

Help me to remember as I compose my stories that you have also created someone to read them. It might be only one person, but use me Father as your instrument to reach them. Use me to my fullest potential.

I am answering your call, Father. I am willing to use my gift to share your love with others.

Amen

Photo credit: Sara Lesire

Do not be anxious about anything, but in every situation, by prayer and petition, with thanksgiving, present your requests to God. And the peace of God, which transcends all understanding, will guard your hearts and your minds in Christ Jesus.
~Philippians 4: 6-7 (NIV)

Heavenly Father,

It's happened. You've trusted me enough to have given me a contract. Now the worry takes over. Can I write this book? On time? Will my writing embarrass you?

How will I balance this work with taking care of my family and spending time with you? My stomach aches from the "what ifs." Will I have to do book signings? Speak in front of a crowd? Please give me the tools I need and chase this anxiety to the ends of the earth.

I am so thankful that I can sit at your feet and tell you my fears. I am calmer now because of that. Thank you, Father, for the blessing of your Son who also knew the pain of anxiety.

Amen

Photo credit: Sara Lesire

Don't let anyone look down on you because you are young, but set an example for the believers in speech, in conduct, in love, in faith and in purity. ~1 Timothy 4:12 (NIV)

Heavenly Father,

There is so much to learn about writing. How will I ever understand it all? So many other authors I know have been writing longer, and they know so much more. Some days the words won't come, or they come in a sloppy mess. Am I rushing this journey? Do I need to spend more time learning?

Please put people in my path who can help me become a writer worthy of this gift you have given to me. I only want to please you and not those of this world.

Father, I also ask for wisdom to use my time wisely. Help me organize my day, thoughts, and actions in a manner pleasing to you.

Amen

Then Samson's wife threw herself on him, sobbing, "You hate me! You don't really love me. You've given my people a riddle, but you haven't told me the answer."

"I haven't even explained it to my father or mother," he replied, "so why should I explain it to you?" She cried the whole seven days of the feast. So on the seventh day he finally told her, because she continued to press him. She in turn explained the riddle to her people.
~Judges 14:16-17 (NIV)

Dear Lord,

In the journey you've given me, please grant me a discerning heart. Help me to recognize the distraction of manipulation whether by guilt or threat or the promise of something sweet. Help me to balance my responsibility to complete the tasks you've given me and avoid the inappropriate response to act on someone else's emotions or desires. Help me to be loving but firm in refusing to accept manipulative behavior from others—or myself toward others.

In Jesus name,

Amen

Since you are my rock and my fortress, for the sake of your name lead and guide me.
~Psalm 31: 3 (NIV)

Dear Lord,

Sometimes I get so caught up in the busy stuff of life that I am distracted easily from the path you've created for me to follow. Then I feel guilty and unworthy. Please help me to be more open to your leading, less distracted, and less condemning of myself. Keep me on your path no matter where it leads.

In Jesus' name,

Amen

As pressure and stress bear down on me, I find joy in your commands.
~Psalm 119:143 (NLT)

Dear Lord,

You already know all that's been, is, and is to come. You already know me. That's amazing and just wow! Help me to focus on you, your plan, and your heart. I get easily lost in it all. But this season is nothing new. It comes each year. Help me to learn this time the things I need to know so I plan better for future seasons. There's no reason for me to be stressed in the normal. But my lack of planning makes it harder. Tuck away in my heart what I need to capture as lessons and wisdom so I'm no longer surprised by what's already known.

In Jesus' name,

Amen

I praise you because I am fearfully and wonderfully made; your works are wonderful, I know that full well.
~Psalm 139:14 (NIV)

Dear Lord,

Sometimes I wonder why I am here—and not there. You know, at this point in my life and career, not as good as... Sometimes I wonder why it seems so easy for everyone else, but not me. Sometimes I wonder why life is so full of struggle, why I trip when someone else sails over that same obstacle.

I know you made me, crafted my purpose, and will lead me even as I wonder what my next step should be. And so, I give you all my "wonder." What will you do with me, Lord? How will you use those many stumbling moments? I wonder...

In Jesus' name,

Amen

Forget the former things; do not dwell on the past. See, I am doing a new thing! Now it springs up; do you not perceive it? I am making a way in the wilderness and streams in the wasteland.
~Isaiah 43:18-19 (NIV)

Dear Lord,

Sometimes I don't think I'm worthy to write. Why do I have anything special to say that hasn't been said before? Why would anyone read it? I feel like I'm always in a wasteland...always waiting. And that waiting makes me feel unworthy, abandoned, lost. Help me to forget those feelings and focus on the things you want me to see. Help me to understand and rejoice in the new things you are doing in my imagination, future, and life. Help me to see the way you are making in my wilderness.

In Jesus' name,

Amen

So that Christ may dwell in your hearts through faith. And I pray that you, being rooted and established in love, may have power, together with all the Lord's holy people, to grasp how wide and long and high and deep is the love of Christ, and to know this love that surpasses knowledge — that you may be filled to the measure of all the fullness of God.
~Ephesians 3:17-19 (NIV)

Dear Lord,

There are people I love, not even strangers, who refuse you. People who are either angry with you or think they're so smart they don't need you. Please open their hearts and minds to you. Please help my writing to open hearts to you. Maybe my characters' flaws or overcoming or forgiveness opens a crack in the wall of the hearts of those who refuse you. Maybe the plot or situation or a line you give me to write touches a nerve. Somehow, please use my writing to open not only strangers' hearts, but those close to me I am so scared will reject you. Please, God of all power and communication and love—love my loved ones and readers into heaven.

In Jesus' name,

Amen

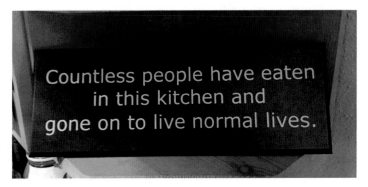

Keep your roots deep in him, build your lives on him, and become stronger in your faith, as you were taught. And be filled with thanksgiving.
~Colossians 2:7 (GNT)

Dear Lord,

Chaos keeps me from doing my best. Sometimes it's of my own making. Sometimes it's beyond my control. Sometimes I start the chaos because I just know life will be much better afterwards, like coping during remodeling a kitchen or rebuilding after a disaster.

But how disruptive and frustrating the work is in my life to reach that goal. I can't see the way through anymore. Help me to keep close to you so you can guide me through the chaos.

In Jesus' name,

Amen

For even when we were with you, we gave you this rule: "The one who is unwilling to work shall not eat."
~2 Thessalonians 3:10 (NIV)

Dear Lord,

Sometimes I get scared. Scared I can't write anything but drivel. Scared no one will like my words. Scared I'm not worthy. So sometimes I avoid or make excuses or get easily distracted from the work of writing.

I ask you to help me through those times so that I may conquer my fear and write as you have made me to do. I ask you to help me do the work of writing so that I may sit at the banquet table and eat the fruit of my labors. I ask that you help me keep my mind on the work you have prepared for me each day, one day at a time.

In Jesus' name,

Amen

Photo credit: D. Cain

Let the words of my mouth and the meditation of my heart be acceptable in your sight, O Lord, my rock and my redeemer.
~Psalm 19:14 (ESV)

Dear Lord, my Rock and my Redeemer,

May the words on my lips and the thoughts of my heart please you. May you find them to be a pleasing and acceptable fragrance. You have blessed me with this ability. May it be that I would use this talent to write in a way that honors and glorifies you. Help me to remember that I'm not writing for fame or fortune, but for you. Through me and my words, may you receive all the praise and be highly exalted.

In your Son's holy name,

Amen

Photo credit: D. Cain

So shall my word be that goes out from my mouth; it shall not return to me empty, but it shall accomplish that which I purpose, and shall succeed in the thing for which I sent it.
~Isaiah 55:11 (ESV)

Dear Father in heaven,

Thank you for the wonderful promises that you have given in your word, abundant encouragement to each who struggles in this life. I praise you that your promises never fail and that you are always faithful to them. Thank you for the strength to accomplish what you have set before me. I pray that you would use my words to accomplish your ends. Help me to remember that the angels in heaven rejoice over even one life touched and transformed. Whatever your purposes for my work, whether big or small, may they bear much fruit for your kingdom.

In your Son's name I pray,

Amen

Photo credit: D. Cain

You did not choose me, but I chose you and appointed you that you should go and bear fruit and that your fruit should abide, so that whatever you ask the Father in my name, he may give it to you.
~John 15:16 (ESV)

Dear Father,

I thank you for choosing me for this task of writing that you've set before me. It's a great responsibility, and sometimes a heavy load to bear. I don't know if I'm up to the job you've given me to do. Please, equip me with all of the tools I need to write for your glory and honor, and for your glory and honor alone. May my work truly produce good fruit in myself and in all of my readers, that lives will be touched with the gospel because of my writing. And, may my fruit abide and produce a harvest of everlasting life.

In your Son's precious name,

Amen

Photo credit: D. Cain

I can do all things through him who strengthens me.
~Philippians 4:13 (ESV)

Dear Heavenly Father,

Thank you for the strength you give to me for each day you have set out before me. On my own, I'm unable to lift a finger or take a breath. I cannot write a single word or produce a single page without you. With you and through you, I can face any circumstance. Whether publication, rejection, criticism, or praise lies before me, please give me the fortitude to face it. Be with me, by my side. Uphold me and remind me of your presence. Thank you for walking this path with me. Thank you for not abandoning me but for supporting me along this path. May I never turn my face from you but always look to you for everything. Provide me the grace and strength I require for this journey.

In your Son's precious name,

Amen

God chose what is low and despised in the world, even things that are not, to bring to nothing things that are, so that no human being might boast in the presence of God.
~1 Corinthians 1:28-29 (ESV)

My Father,

What am I, that you should choose me for the task you've set before me, to write these stories you've placed on my heart? You haven't chosen the strong or the wise, but the weak and the low, the ones the world deems foolish. Thank you for this calling you have given me, for this privilege and responsibility. May my only boast be in you, for there is nothing greater of which to boast. It is you who gives the desire, you who gives the talent, you who gives the stories. My boast is that you've blessed me in this way. Use my words to bring glory and honor to your name.

In Christ alone,

Amen

To this end we always pray for you, that our God may make you worthy of his calling and may fulfill every resolve for good and every work of faith by his power, so that the name of our Lord Jesus may be glorified in you, and you in him, according to the grace of our God and the Lord Jesus Christ.
~2 *Thessalonians 1:11-12 (ESV)*

Dear Lord,

When troubles and trials come in my life and in my writing, help me to remember that the purpose of this gift is to glorify you and to honor you. Bless me in this calling, Lord, and help me to walk by faith. Increase my resolve to do my best for you, to not get distracted by the world and by the things going on around me. Fill me with your grace, for that is what sustains me. And in the end, whether I experience success or failure as the world judges it, may you receive all the honor, because you alone are truly worthy.

In Jesus' name,

Amen

Now may the God of peace who brought again from the dead our Lord Jesus, the great shepherd of the sheep, by the blood of the eternal covenant, equip you with everything good that you may do his will, working in us that which is pleasing in his sight, through Jesus Christ, to whom be glory forever and ever. Amen
~Hebrews 13:20-21 (ESV)

Dear Father of peace,

Please grant me the peace I need to know that you are working out everything to your perfect will. Bless my writing Lord, and use it in the way that you see fit. Equip me with everything I need to write, to speak your words, to touch lives for you. Thank you for the gift of your Son, my righteousness, who can take what is broken, even the words I put to paper, and make it beautiful.

In the Savior's name,

Amen

And even the very hairs of your head are all numbered. So don't be afraid;
you are worth more than many sparrows.
~Matthew 10:30-31 (NIV)

Dear Heavenly Father,

In the midst of so much rejection it is easy to feel unworthy of anything, let alone a calling. Yet your word says you value me. Not for what I can do for you but simply because you love me.

You know the intimate details of my life. You know my heart's desires, for you planted them there. And you know the road I must walk, the journey I must take to nurture those desires and make them wholly yours.

Help me to not get discouraged but to trust in your plan for me, to rest in being beloved by you.

In your Son's precious name,

Amen

I consider that our present sufferings are not worth comparing with the glory that will be revealed in us.
~Romans 8:18 (NIV)

Dear Lord,

I am so easily caught up in my own present circumstances. I readily see what is wrong and what I would like changed and tell you often how I wish things were different. And yet I have the barest inkling of the glory that is yet to come. That my present circumstances won't even compare to what you have in store for me.

It is so easy to be discouraged when my eyes are on the waves crashing around me. But remind me who created the waves, who bids them to be still. Remind me to keep my eyes, my focus on you and what you have in store for me. Because it is good. Because you are good, and you give good gifts whether or not our earthly eyes can always see it.

In Jesus' name,

Amen

As a prisoner for the Lord, then, I urge you to live a life worthy of the calling you have received.
~Ephesians 4:1 (NIV)

Dear God,

You have called me out of darkness into your amazing light through the gift of your Son. But so often I focus on myself instead of my calling. Instead of exhibiting fruit of the Spirit, I exhibit anger, hatred, divisiveness, discontent, impatiences, hurtfulness, and discord.

I am a daughter of the King, of the Creator of the universe who has chosen me to do his work. What an amazing gift! And yet so often I become consumed and distracted by my humanity and sinfulness.

Help me to remember that to which you have called me. Help me to act in a worthy manner. Help me to reflect your love to all those around me, particularly my fellow brothers and sisters in the faith.

In the name of Jesus,

Amen

Whatever happens, conduct yourselves in a manner worthy of the gospel of Christ. Then, whether I come and see you or only hear about you in my absence, I will know that you stand firm in the one Spirit, striving together as one for the faith of the gospel...
~Philippians 1:27 (NIV)

Dear Heavenly Father,

It can be so easy to get caught up in competition and in comparison. I can easily let someone else's successes steal my joy when they achieve something I have not. My focus is so easily distracted and placed on myself and others instead of where it belongs: on you. I can be so caught up in myself and in competition that I forget that I should be striving together with my brothers and sisters in Christ toward the gospel, not myself.

Help me to conduct myself worthy of that which you have called me to, the wonderful privilege of a relationship with you. Convict me when my actions are not honoring to you.

In your Son's name,

Amen

What is more, I consider everything a loss because of the surpassing worth of knowing Christ Jesus my Lord, for whose sake I have lost all things. I consider them garbage, that I may gain Christ...
~*Philippians 3:8 (NIV)*

Dear Jesus,

My desire for achievement here on earth can seem so precious to me. Getting an agent, getting a book contract, winning a contest or an award, having good sales, making a bestseller list. And those aren't bad things. They can be good gifts from you in the right circumstances.

But when compared to what you did for me on the cross so I could know you as a friend and savior, they are absolutely nothing. Help me to keep everything in its proper perspective. Help me to never lose sight of the precious gift you've given me in yourself.

In your precious name,

Amen

[S]o that you may live a life worthy of the Lord and please him in every way: bearing fruit in every good work, growing in the knowledge of God...
~Colossians 1:10 (NIV)

Dear Lord God,

I want to please you with my writing, with my actions, with my life. I want to bear good fruit. But it can be so hard in this world where image is everything and the deeper things are not valued.

Not only do I want to grow in the knowledge of my craft, but I want to grow in my knowledge of you. I spend so much time learning and practicing my craft. Do I give my relationship with you equal importance?

Show me how to keep my focus on you, how to walk in Your path, how to develop the fruit in my life that is pleasing to You.

In Jesus' name,

Amen

These have come so that the proven genuineness of your faith—of greater worth than gold, which perishes even though refined by fire—may result in praise, glory and honor when Jesus Christ is revealed.
~1 Peter 1:7 (NIV)

Abba Father,

No one likes to go through trials. Sometimes the whole business of writing seems like one trial after another: learning the craft, putting my work before others, getting feedback and rejection. Some of it makes me stronger, better, more refined as a writer and as a person. But some of it is just painful.

Help me to discern the truth of others' words. Guide me with your still, small voice on your path. Remind me daily that your light shining through me is the refinement I'm striving for, and that your glory, praise, and honor is the ultimate goal, not my own. Thank you for your loving patience with me as I grow and learn.

In your Son's name,

Amen

Rather, it should be that of your inner self, the unfading beauty of a gentle and quiet spirit, which is of great worth in God's sight.
~1 Peter 3:4 (NIV)

Dear God,

As a person who has a rich inner life and can entertain myself with my own thoughts and imagination, it can be easy for me to think that I have a gentle and quiet spirit.

And yet, I need to examine myself closely. Where do I have thoughts of comparison, of anger, even of jealousy? While these might not always be evident on the outside, they are not the fruit of the gentle and quiet spirit. That only comes from resting in you, from allowing you to direct my path, and trusting in your plan for my life.

When I am tempted to compare myself with others and become discouraged, gently focus my eyes back on you.

In Jesus' name,

Amen

Father God,
Bless the reader of this book, fill their worthy cup until it
overflows.
Bless the reader of the book.
Bless the reader of this book.
Bless the reader of the book.

~The Pencildancers

Here are the Christian book samples we promised. If you've
never read Christian fiction or nonfiction before, here's a
chance to test it out. If you have read these kinds of books,
consider a few new ones by the authors of *Worthy to Write*.
Enjoy!

The Honey Bride by Diana Lesire Brandmeyer

May 1887, Trenton, Illinois

Wind-whipped water plopped on, splattered, and then moistened Katie Tucker's forehead, rousing her. Something wasn't right. She'd fallen asleep with open windows, hoping for a breeze to relieve the early summer heat. Now the wind was wicked, pulsating against the bedroom panes and blowing in rain. She sat, reached for the window, and closed it with a bang.

The sky lit up once, twice. The hair on her arms stretched for heaven. Crack. The second story sizzled and popped. Lightning. She shivered. Was it a tornado, like the one she'd read about last month? Five people in Wabash County had died.

Papa would be yelling to go the cellar any minute. Please, God, not down there. Chill bumps raced up her arms.

Henry, her younger brother, banged against her door and called out, jarring her from the nightmare of spider webs stuck in her hair.

Had he said fire? In the house? The barn? Shaking, she fumbled for her wrapper, found it, then rushed her arms through the sleeves. Her shoes were by the back door. Henry waited at the bottom of the stairs.

"The barn's on fire. Papa's out there."

"Get a bucket! I'll get the stew pan. Where's Oma?"

"Sleeping."

"I'll wake her. Get as many things filled with water as you can." Henry's boots pounded sharply against the wood floor in time to her heart beat. She needed to wake her grandmother.

Oma met her at the doorway.

"What's the yelling about?"

"Lightning started a fire in the barn. Papa is getting out the animals. I was coming to wake you."

"I'm up. Go help. I'll be there as soon as possible."

Katie hesitated. Should she insist her grandmother stay inside?

"Go, Schatzi. Now."

Her grandmother's strong words urged her feet forward and she hightailed it down the stairs. She trembled on the bench, trying to get her shaking fingers to work her laces into place. The unnatural noises from the animals made her want to run back to bed. No matter how fearful she was she couldn't. There was work to be done.

Outside, the smoke lay heavy in the air. They needed help. The farmhand Papa hired hadn't shown up. If they could get word to the fire department, but they were too far from town. She'd send Henry to the Gibbons'. They were the closest.

Henry worked the pump, water pouring, splashing against the bucket sides.

"Where's Papa?"

"Still in there. He got Starlight out first."

"Good. Get on her, ride to the Gibbons', and tell them we need help."

"I can help."

"We need more than the three of us. Hurry. You're faster than me."

Henry ran for the horse. Katie picked up the bucket of water Henry had filled. The handles bit into her hands as she carried it to the barn. "Papa! I have water!"

"I'm here." He grabbed the bucket and ran inside. Seconds later he was back. "Fill it again. Hurry." He coughed. "Where's Henry?"

"I sent him for help." Flames licked the inside of the dry barn wood.

"They won't make it before it's burned to the ground." Her father bent over coughing. When he was able to catch his breath, he handed her his kerchief. "Wet that and bring it with the next bucket. Lady Jane is still in there."

She shuddered. Lady Jane was difficult on a good day. In a fire, who knew what the horse was capable of doing.

***

Unable to sleep, Pete Dent paced the Gibbons' barn, where he slept. The rhythm of the rain didn't bring its usual soothing. Storms didn't bother him, but this one did. Too soon, too dangerous, after the one last month. He stood in the open door and noticed Roy standing on the porch. He jogged across the yard and up the steps. "Thunder keeping you awake?"

"Scared Frances. Alma's taking care of her." Roy said.

Crack. The lightening startled both men.

"That was close. Sounded like it hit something." Roy ran to the edge of the porch.

Pete looked the other way, toward the Tucker place. Katie on his mind, again. He'd like to get to know her better. It had taken him a few months, but he'd managed to get her to smile at him at church anyway. Shy little thing. He'd been ready to pull up stakes and find another place to work when she'd caught his eye. Katie might be the one person to tip the scale and keep him in Trenton.

"Do you see that?" Roy pointed in the direction Pete had been staring.

"That's a bright light. Too bright. Think they got hit with that last bolt?" Pete's heart pounded. "I'm riding out. They might need help if it hit the house or barn."

"Go. I'll let Alma know and meet you."

Pete wasted no time saddling Biscuit and urging him to a gallop. As he grew closer to the Tucker's, he knew something was burning. Probably the barn with the way the flames were flicking the sky. Someone rode toward him. Katie coming for help? He slowed his horse.

"Hey, our barn's on fire. Can you help?"

"Henry, is that you?"

"Yeah, Pete. Katie told me get you. Hurry! Papa's getting the animals out and. . ." Henry stopped to catch his breath.

"I heard you. That's where I'm headed. Roy's behind me."

Henry turned Starlight around.

Both horses stretched into a neck-to-neck race for the Tucker barn.

When they arrived, the smoke was thick, but the bright flames licked through, illuminating the night, revealing Katie lugging a bucket. Pete dismounted and tied Biscuit to the porch railing. He ran to Katie and pried her fingers from the handle. "Fill another one and keep filling. I'll get them to the barn. Roy's on his way."

"Papa's in there! I can't get to him."

Cold sweat tickled down his back. If Mr. Tucker was still in that barn, the odds were he wasn't coming out. Please, God, let her father be alive. He ran inside, keeping low. "Mr. Tucker! Holler your position!" The roaring flames sucked his words into silence. He tossed the water on a bale of hay and ran out, gasping for air.

Katie waited with a pan of water. He took it and rushed back inside. He had to find her father.

***

Katie sat on the back steps, hugging Henry close to her. Waiting. Most of their church congregation either stood in the yard or were in the house. Katie and Henry sat alone. She couldn't talk to anyone, not even Alma.

Pete Dent had been kind, explaining how her father probably inhaled too much smoke and couldn't breathe. He'd seen it before, serving on the volunteer fire department. He told her to take Henry inside, but she couldn't. If she left these steps, it would be real. So she clung to Henry and waited.

Tears rolled down her cheeks, bringing some relief to the sting from the smoke.

Meet Diana Lesire Brandmeyer

CBA and ECPA bestselling, Christian author, Diana Lesire Brandmeyer, writes historical and contemporary romances about women choosing to challenge their fears to become the strong woman God intends. Author of *Mind of Her Own, A Time to Dance, We're Not Blended We're Pureed, A Survivor's Guide to Blended Families.*

Website/blog: www.DianaBrandmeyer.com
Facebook: dianalesirebrandmeyerauthor
Twitter: @dianabrandmeyer
Instagram: dianabrandmeyer

Books by Diana:

Contemporary
A Time to Dance
A Time to Bake
Mind of Her Own
Hearts on the Road

Historical
From a Distance
The Festive Bride
The Honey Bride

Matchmaker Brides Collection
Rails to Love Collection

Children
The Trouble with Ralph
The Smithton Necklace Mystery

Nonfiction
We're Not Blended, We're Pureed: a Survivor's Guide to Blended Families

Chapter 4, from *Gems of Wisdom*
by Angela Breidenbach

Courage
Gemstone: Obsidian
Pirates: Fear and Short-term Thinking.

The LORD says, 'I will guide you along the best pathway
for your life. I will advise you and watch over you.'
   —Psalm 32:8 (NLT)

Snowflakes bursting against a night sky—the perfect
description of the snowflake obsidian's white splash on gray
rock. Sometimes the flakes overlap and create patches of
snow. It's a natural glass sculpture that looks like an artist
intended to create one-of-a-kind abstract pieces. Obsidian
is formed deep within volcanoes and erupts to the top crust.
Because it cools quickly, obsidian's composition is finer than
the water-filled and slower, deep cooling magma that be-
comes granite. One thing to fear about any piece of obsidian,
particularly for the unaware, is its sharpness. It can cut skin
easily. The danger is real.

Record your answers to questions in the following sec-
tions in Chapter 4 of the Companion Guide.

Ponder Point: John
A delicate hand with short little fingers pulled on my
shirt. Tugging hard, she demanded my attention. "Daddy, I
don't know what to do."

"Sure you do. You talked about this." I ruffled her hair.

She stared up at me, not a simple, wondering stare but a
long how-could-you-throw-me-to-the-wolves stare. I almost
caved. Almost.

"Honey, you practiced." I had visions of after dinner
memorization for the last week. "You worked hard on this. I

know you can do it."

That's when she caved. I know she didn't mean to. I thought her lunge forward was an escape attempt. I caught her around the hips in time to swing her back toward the stage—and toward me.

My mistake. My shoes were baptized with undigested tacos. I sighed as I smelled her fear. Now I really had to help her make this speech happen.

I squish, squish, squished her over to the women's bathroom door. "In you go. I'll be back."

Squish, squish, I looked down and grimaced. Squish, squish. One long sigh escaped. I took off my shoes—and socks—and held them at arm's length as I walked into the men's room, where they landed in the garbage. I needed new loafers anyway.

She stood by the water fountain, waiting for me and my freshly washed feet. Her eyes went wide at my Fred Flintstone appearance. "Sorry, Daddy." And she burst into tears.

Humbled by an eight-year old, I knelt down and folded her into my arms, clipping the water fountain handle with my funny bone. I choked back a grunt. Man that smarts!

"Can we go home now?"

"Sweetie, I love you. Because I love you, I'm going to help you through this."

She sounded like a wounded animal against my neck. "Please."

"Nope." I pulled back from the hug. "Do you know why?"

She shook her head without looking up from the button on my shirt. Crystal tears clung to her lashes. I gulped.

"Because you did the homework. All that effort, you deserve to show it off. Think about how good you're going to feel when you recite such a pretty poem."

"It's pretty?"

"Very pretty, especially the way you say it. How sad I'd be if I didn't get to see you."

"You'd really be sad?" She looked forlorn. She didn't

want to disappoint me. But it wasn't about disappointment for me. It was about teaching one little girl I love to overcome her fears.

"Could you practice one more time right here?"

She nodded. "Okay."

"How does it go?"

I wondered if the teacher picked that poem knowing my little girl's personality or if it was one she had the class do each year.

She chanted the well-known piece in a staccato singsong while picking out a ceiling tile for her audience of one.

Today, upon a bus,
I saw a girl with golden hair,
And wished I was as fair.
When suddenly, she rose to leave,
I saw her hobble down the aisle.
She had one leg and wore a crutch.
But as she passed, she gave a smile.

Oh God, forgive me when I whine.
I have two legs, the world is mine . . .

She stopped. Her eyes slid from the ceiling tile to the wall as if she were thinking.

Had she forgotten it? Was she going to cry? Had I pushed too hard?

And then she stood a little taller. When she looked back at me, she smiled.

I nodded for her to finish the last three verses.

Her voice grew stronger as her confidence burst forth from deep within like magma cooling into fine obsidian, smooth and unique. No longer singsong, but with a sweet, emphatic lilt, she told the story, and it became her own.

I saw the miracle happen, standing in the hallway barefoot, the way the earth creates a sculpture. I saw her personality crystallize right in front of me, as individual as a snowflake. I saw words of an anonymous writer speak into her. She "got it," and the whole meaning clicked. She had survived this metamorphosis.

Fred Flintstone and I have a lot in common. His gushy cartoon pride in Pebbles could be drawn from my own face, while I held my bruised elbow, mesmerized.

With feet to take me where I'd go.
With eyes to see the sunset's glow.
With ears to hear what I would know.
Oh God, forgive me when I whine.
I've been blessed indeed, the world is mine.

She threw her arms wide and grinned. "Daddy, I'm blessed, huh?"

"Yes, you sure are. Do you think it's time to bless someone else?"

I padded after my eight-year-old as she ran backstage. I stubbed my toe on something in the dark. Hopping back and forth, I had a lot in common with Fred! But the bumps and bruises were worth it all because, against all odds, my Pebbles learned something that would matter for life. I had the tiniest part in guiding her to reach deep inside and face her fears. I'm blessed, indeed.

Pique Points
- What do you do with fears that intense?
- What could inspire us to step out in faith?
- Do you recognize encouragement from others as a blessing?

Personal Place: Angie's Story

Inside the swimming dome, the artificial weather held the temperature at a steady, comfortable level. Inside my head, I knew it was still way below freezing outside. Why did I sign up for this class again? Oh yeah, right, I knew how to swim and this was an easy A.

I looked at the skylights. Heavy snow muffled out the daylight. Darkness felt like night. A chill skimmed across my body. If the swimming suit I wore could only be a coat. Instead, the spandex and polyester felt more like a second skin and showed every goose bump—bumps everywhere that made me look like a diseased chicken instead of a high school swimmer. I stared at the water.

"Let's go! Four laps to warm up." The P.E. teacher's whistle blew. The first group dove.

"Sadist." I whispered as my bare feet absorbed winter from the tiles. I walked to the deep end, but not to the edge. The smothered skylight held my fascination. What if the snow crashed through and fell into the pool? What if the blizzard outside broke through the windows? My eyes followed the leadership of my thoughts. The windows. Up high and fogged with ice. I shivered again as the whistle squawked in my ear.

A gap, not too big—okay too big—yawned between me and the deep end. The last group of swimmers hit the water with a slap, slap, splash. I had to step up. But knowing how to swim—and willingly jumping into cold water in the middle of a snowstorm? Two different things. My long hair would take forever to dry. I'd probably get an ear infection or something. Stupid decision with my tendency for ear infections.

Shadows darkened the middle of the pool. Snow shadows. Big, huge blobs of shadow hid the bottom. What was I thinking? Knowing how to swim and knowing how to twist and flip from the high dive—way different things.

What was I thinking? It looked easy on TV when lithe Olympians arced through the air. I love the grace and beauty of the freefall. I peered at the high dive. Was it really that high? Chicken skin covered every inch of me. I rubbed hard on my forearms. Think warm thoughts. Caribbean, Mexico, warm water . . . cliff divers . . . high divers . . . I shuddered.

The picture of Dana Kunze making the 172-foot world record high dive popped into my mind. What was that diving board? I looked at it again. Twenty feet? I can do this. I want to do this. I want to learn to dive. It's not like 172 feet. All I have to do is warm up first.

Mr. Sadistic noticed my hesitation. I hung my head and took a deep breath. Here it comes.

He leaned in close. Close enough that I could smell mint from his toothpaste. "You know how to swim, right?"

I nodded, not taking my eyes off the gray speckled tiles. I hadn't even made it to the white ones ringing the pool.

"Then all you have to do right now is what you already know. Jump in and give me four laps."

"I'm cold."

"Yep. Go warm up. After four laps, you'll wonder why there's no AC in here."

"Yeah?" I looked at the ladder to my right. I couldn't help myself.

"Trust me." He tossed his head toward the tower. "You'll deal with that later. Just take it one thing at a time."

"Okay. Swim, right?"

"Right. And it always helps me to count."

"Count." I dared to look him in the eye. "Like one, two, three?"

He stepped back and yelled, "One . . . two . . . " Then nothing. He stood there issuing the challenge in front of fifteen other high schoolers.

Sadistic. "Three." I ran the few steps forward and leapt. My arms swept forward as I flew off the side of the pool, toes pointed and perfect. Absolutely perfect. And I knew it.

I knew everyone watched me fly.

I knew he watched.

I knew, too, he knew that dive was perfect form.

That's what terrified me.

I hadn't meant to impress him. Instinct had taken over. I'd been side diving since kindergarten. I kicked hard to the shallow end, pulverizing the water as if it were my brain. Dumb. So dumb! So dumb! My arms sliced hard into each pull.

Mr. Sadistic would now expect perfection from me because he knew I could do it. I could dive off the side of a pool in a stratospheric, gorgeous front dive. I could do a phenomenal back dive too. Ask me for a pretty side dive, voilà, you'll get one—but only off the side of the pool.

What I couldn't do was any dive off the high board. Now Mr. Expectant would hold me up in front of the rest of the class as an example. His expectations would be higher than the high board he was supposed to teach. What was I thinking?

Three more laps. I flip-turned and swam hard. Somewhere around the middle of lap three, I realized how warm my body felt. I relaxed into the crawl stroke. The ease of movement lulled me into a better mood as I finished the last length.

"Line up. Everyone jump three times off the springboard. Feet first. No running take-off."

Ok-a-a-a-y. Kind of like kindergarten, playtime. I could do that. The three-step ladder's metal ridges poked the bottoms of my feet. The board felt better, though rough like sandpaper.

I'm walking—I'm walking—splash. I knew a grin split my face like a jack-o-lantern. It was fun to drop right into the water. I did it twice more. I'd become last in everything. I didn't mind. Maybe I could run around and jump in one more time before class ended.

The whistle blew. "Over here. You're going to learn proper take off for the spring board."

We practiced the technique on the deck together like a dance team.

"Now on the low board."

The class scrambled into line.

I began to shiver. Instead of backing away from the cold water, I found myself longing to jump in. I knew the water would feel warmer now. I jogged in place.

"Three times each. Go in feet first."

Well, if it went like this, I'd be fine. Then I caught a flicker out of the corner of my eye; the high board loomed over me. It didn't have a three-step ladder. I swallowed. One . . . Two . . . Three . . . and I flew off the end of the low board headfirst.

I heard the whistle underwater and all the way to the surface.

"You showing off?"

"Uh, no. Sorry, I wasn't thinking."

"What were you doing?"

"Um, counting."

He nodded. "Seems to work."

I caught the hint of a smile as I took the offered grip up and out of the pool.

He turned to the class and blew a short whistle. "Everyone to the high board."

I heard it then. The collective gasp. My chicken skin erupted. I had itchy hair popping up on my legs even though I'd shaved the night before.

"The only way to conquer fear is to conquer it."

"Yeah, I think you are Mr. Sadistic." I whispered down at my blue feet. The kid next to me heard and snickered.

"Climb and walk off the board." He looked around the group. Several other kids watched the ripples on the surface of the water or the wall or their feet, like me. "Hey, all eyes on me." He waited what seemed like an hour. "Do not stop. Focus on the far wall to keep your perspective. Walk off the end. Keep your arms at your sides and not flapping like a bird. The only way off that board is at that end." He pointed at the long plank hanging over the middle of the water. "Do it three times today, or you flunk."

Flunk? This was supposed to be an easy A. I needed the A. I needed an easy class with my heavy load. I squared my shoulders. Mr. Sadistic would not flunk me. I would not flunk me. Whoa—revelation. I was the one who would choose how this ended. I stepped closer. I did not let the gap happen. I didn't want to be left behind.

The whistle blew. His eyebrows rose in, yep, expectation. He picked up his clipboard and, as each person walked the plank, ticked a mark.

I grasped the silver rails and stepped up. I counted each

step. One, two, three . . . The far wall emerged and captured my attention. I did not stop. Then, ready to place my footing, I looked at the white sandpaper surface. And I stopped. Peripherally, I could see the gray tiles far below. I slid my vision slightly left. The tiles. I stared at the tiles.

A tinny, weak voice said, "Count."

The whistle spurted like an angry rooster. Prrrt. Prrrrrt. Prrrrrrrr!

I jumped and noticed Mr. Sadistic step into my view, right where I'd been staring.

"COUNT!" I heard again.

I blinked a few times.

"Look at that far wall and count!" He shouted from below.

"Oh. Yeah. Count." I nodded. "One." I stepped up. "Two." I walked forward one step. "Three." I walked off the end of the plank. I fell fast. My arms flew up from my sides and slapped hard on the surface. Ow!

I didn't go very deep. My wings had stopped my underwater descent. I surfaced quickly.

"Over here." He called me to the wall. "What are you going to do differently next time?"

I looked up at him and then over to watch another kid take the step into emptiness. "I'm going to keep my arms down." I put one hand on red, burning skin to cool it.

"Good. Go."

I hopped out of the pool and lined up for two more leaps.

One long whistle blew as I returned to the breathing world. Diving class ended. "You face your fears by preparation. Preparation starts in your head and moves to your actions. Someone tell me what you've done today to prepare you to leap off that height." He pointed.

I raised my hand. "I started really scared. But you made me take it one step at a time. Then you built up from the pool to the low board to the high board."

He grinned. "Yes, you did. But it goes farther than that.

You made a decision. What was it?"

"I made the decision to jump."

"Exactly. It starts with the decision. Once you've made the decision, you take small steps to learn how to leap."

Those were leaps that stay with me to this day. I learned how to face my fear. I use those skills even when it hurts a little. I learned it didn't hurt enough to stop me. Little things I could tweak would help like keeping my arms at my sides and not staring at the wrong spot. And I still count to get started sometimes rather than stay frozen in my fear.

Psst, thank you, Mr. Sadistic.

Pique Points
- What fear has you frozen right now?
- What skills have you used in the past to handle fearful things?
- Can you take small steps toward what needs to happen?
- Do you have a plan in place, or will you be taken by surprise?

Putting It All Together

Learning to dive or even go near the water causes terror in some people. The fear of heights, speaking in public, spiders—you name it, a fear exists. Taking care of loved ones can be scary, too.

What happens when it's time to take away the keys from an elderly driver? What happens when you don't agree with a doctor? What if they get mad? Those fears are valid. It's easy to doubt our own ability to solve problems. Anger, sharp and dark like obsidian, could cause loved ones to cut us out of their lives.

The coping skills you've used all your life can be helpful now. Like learning to jump into the water, even though you know it's the first step toward climbing the high dive. Counting can help, too, because you are conditioned to act.

Consider mental preparation and practice with a trustworthy friend for the intense moments to come. They will come. That isn't the issue. The question is: How will you handle them when they do?

Pirates

"I don't need to be doin' this, lovey. All ya has to do is gimme what I be wantin' now." The pirate held a branding iron over bright orange and yellow flames.

The governor's daughter cringed, her torn silk dress singed from the bonfire already. "What do you want?"

"A pretty maid likes of you's smart, aren't ya, lassie?" He came so close to whisper the last words that her hair curled from the heat of the iron he held up.

"What do you want?" She cried out.

"Nothing much." He winked. "A mere pittance, really."

She couldn't tell if sweat or tears rolled over her cheeks on this hot summer night. She screamed, "WHAT? What do you want?"

"Now, now. No cause for alarm." He patted her arm while holding the metal close enough to turn her delicate skin red without touching a freckle. "I'll set you free poppet. Just tell me where yer papa keeps the keys so's me and me maties can free the good Cap'n. We aren't out to harm ye, little lady; we're wantin' a treasure."

"You'd let me go?"

"Ah, poppet, I wouldn't lie . . ." His eyes flickered in the firelight.

Remember.

Remember that pirates are liars.

But by now, you know that the pirates are on the rampage. You've been preparing for situations like this. There are multiple angles and opportunities to this reality. These pirates are trying to take what they don't own. Alerted to the surprise attack, now preempt it by preparing a plan.

The Pirates of Fear and Short-Term Thinking know how to make us focus on a branding iron held to the fire. You think you know what that will do. You believe you cannot handle the torture these pirates will dish out. In order to avoid the perceived pain, you'll take the promise of no pain, sometimes even when you know it is a lie.

Or will you?

Polishing Point

"I am/was terrified about having children and passing on this disease." Nina's comment echoes feelings that occur frequently in families that have hereditary medical conditions. How do you get past fears like this or fear of heights or even the fear to speak up?

Prepare. The best way to face fear is to be offensive and not defensive. Take the time to explore what's coming in the near future. Explore through conversation and make notes. It's too hard to remember later. Jot down questions during the conversation, especially if there's no answer, for later action.

Expect to face the fear. The timing may surprise us, but it will come.

Assess what you know. Where are you right now in the situation? Do you know enough about what you fear, of the expectation itself?

Referrals. Look for someone who has gone through the situation. Most people love to help others and love to share opinions on what worked and what didn't. Start asking for referrals and then act on them. Make a coffee date. Listen to someone else's experiences. Use whatever you can glean from several different people. Don't assume that you'll get all you need from one person.

Sketch out a plan. No one can remember everything they plan. Get organized and sketch it out on paper in the form of an outline, freehand notes, or even a drawing. Put down anything that creates a firm visual or solid understanding of the idea. The more you understand, the more confident you'll feel. The more confident you feel, the more likely you'll act on the information. Those pirates of fear and short-term thinking will have no power when you preempt the strike.

PEARS. Prepare, Expect, Assess, Referrals, Sketch.

***

In honor of your new resolves, claim the obsidian as a gemstone of wisdom on your treasure hunt by saying the following out loud.

This obsidian represents courage as it bursts forth from deep within me. I will use the sharp edges of my fear to sculpt this unique gemstone of wisdom. I will practice preparing, expecting, assessing, and getting referrals to sketch out a polished plan.

Get your copy and read *Gems of Wisdom: The Treasure of Experience* by Angela Breidebach today.

Meet Angela Breidenbach

Angela Breidenbach is a bestselling author of fiction through the ages with most of her books set in Montana. She's the host of Lit Up! on TogiNet.com and iTunes about great entertainment from books to movies.

The Melody of the Soul
Music of Hope Series, Book One

A WWII women's fiction novel by Liz Tolsma

Prologue
Prague, February 1943

Anna Zadoková held her mother's tiny body close. If only she could imprint the feel of her on her skin. She breathed in her scent, a combination of rose water and fried onions. Everything she loved best about her. A light mist dampened them both.

"Be a good girl, beruško."

"No, Máma, ne." She peered over Máma's shoulder and stared at her father. "Ne, Táta. I'm going with you. My deportation notice might not have come with yours, but it will come at some point. The entire family must go together. We won't allow them to separate us."

"And what about your grandmother?" Máma smoothed Anna's hair from her damp brow. "It's a blessing from God that neither of you got your notices. For now, you're safe. You can take care of Babička, and we can go in peace, knowing she'll be looked after."

Anna bit her trembling lip to keep away the tears clogging her throat. "Please, let me go with you. Over the years, we prayed together, laughed together, cried together. This, too, we should do together." Her heart drummed against her ribs with the knowledge of what she faced, what her decision might cost her. She turned and surveyed her younger sisters, Jana and Lada, standing to the side, clutching the two bags allowed them by the Germans.

Prague's exhibition hall loomed behind them, the large wooden structure nothing more than a run-down shack. Other Jews filled the yard, eyes wide, faces drawn. Outside, flimsy wooden partitions separated dozens of toilets. If you had to relieve yourself, you had to do it in full view of everyone present. Anna couldn't say a word. Were the Nazis determined to degrade them?

Máma sighed, dark half-moons beneath her brown eyes. "Ne, ne. If you stay, at least I don't have to worry about you. Or my mother. That's one less burden for me to carry."

Táta stroked Anna's cheek. Deep lines etched his face, lines that hadn't been there before. He took off his hat and rubbed his bald head. "Don't do this to your mother and me. In the middle of the sorrow of leaving everyone and every-thing for an uncertain fate, we're comforted that you and Babička will be safe. Perhaps you will survive. The Americans have joined the fight. Not long now, and they'll be here."

"Táta, I can't survive without my family. I'll die of a bro-ken heart. I, I . . ." She swallowed lest she give up control.

"We can't lose all of our children. David also got his no-tice. He'll be on the train with us. Why you didn't get yours, only the Lord knows. But we believe He did it for a reason."

Anna pursed her lips and set her jaw. "What difference does it make if it comes today or tomorrow? The Nazis want to cleanse Prague of Jews. Even the Christian ones."

Táta flashed her a wry grin. "I have your grandmother to thank for your stubbornness."

"That stubbornness will serve me well in the camp." She locked her knees so her parents wouldn't see her tremble. Should she go home, or go with her family? Her stomach clenched. At least if she went with them, she would have them to help her.

Máma squeezed Anna's hand and stood as straight and regal as ever. "Anna, turn around and go to the house. Now."

Her sister Lada, only eleven years old, cried. "Máma, can't I go home, too? Why do we have to come here?"

Táta rubbed his youngest daughter's shoulder. "This is what God has planned for us. We'll submit to His will and pray for His protection." A muscle worked in his cheek.

Anna clung to him. "We should have gone to America

with Uncle Ivan when we had the chance. We would have been safe. Why did you listen to me? Why did we stay?"

"That wasn't God's plan for us. It's too much to explain now."

But she didn't understand. How could it be His plan for them to be parted this way?

A tall, scrawny young man approached them, his long, black coat flapping in the breeze. Anna gave Jakub Meles, David's friend and a member of the Jewish Council, a half smile.

"What are you doing here?" He finger-combed his unruly black curls.

Táta set down his battered case and patted Anna's hand. "We got our notices to report. We understand that David did, too. Have you seen him?"

"Why is Anna here?" He leaned in, and Anna only heard his words because she stood next to Táta. "You know the council draws up the deportation lists. David begged me, so I had her name and Paní Doubeková's stricken. He was afraid his grandmother wouldn't survive the camp, and he wanted Anna to stay and watch over her. I cannot save her if she shows up here. Send her home."

Táta's drawn face brightened. "God's provision." He gathered Anna to himself like he had hundreds of times when she was a child. "Do as I say. Leave us. Be safe. May the Lord go with you."

The tears, close to the surface all day, streamed down her cheeks in a torrent. "Táta. Oh, Táta."

He held her a moment more before pulling himself from her embrace. Moisture shimmered on his angular face. "This is the hardest thing I have ever done. I have loved you from the moment your mother told me you were on your way. Your tiny face captured my heart and hasn't let it go. My sweet, sweet Anna, my beruško, do this one last thing for me. Go home. Take care of your grandmother."

Her father kissed her cheek, turned her toward their flat on Salvátorská Street, and gave her a gentle push in that direction.

After she walked half a block, she turned back. Her family strolled hand-in-hand into the exhibition hall.

In the distance, a train whistled.

Meet Liz Tolsma

Passionate might best describe Liz Tolsma. She loves writing, research, and editing. Her passion shone through in her first novel which was a double award finalist.

On any given day, you might find her pulling weeds in her perennial garden, walking her hyperactive dog, or curled up with a good book.

Nothing means more to her than her family. She married her high-school sweetheart twenty-nine years ago. Get her talking about international adoption and you might never get her to stop. She and her husband adopted three children, including a son who is a U.S. Marine, and two daughters.

You can find her at www.liztolsma.com where you can sign up for her newsletter for information on her latest releases.

Books by Liz

WWII novels
Snow on the Tulips
Daisies Are Forever
Remember the Lilies

Novellas
Log Cabin Christmas
Rails to Love
Matchmaker Brides
Second Chance Brides

Promise Me by Jennifer Vander Klipp

Orange County, California

The fog was calling. Cait Bellamy lifted her digital SLR camera off the passenger seat of her Jetta. No point in bringing the whole camera bag when she wouldn't use more than the zoom lens already attached. She liked the challenge provided by having only one lens with her. Gravel crunched under her Keds as she stepped out into the parking lot, shutting and locking her car before tucking the keys in her pocket.

Slinging her camera over her shoulder—and freeing her long, blonde hair from under the strap—she passed the Samashima farm store, busy even though it was Valentine's Day. Maybe people were hoping to make last-minute chocolate-covered strawberries from the early producers. Those strawberries weren't nearly as sweet as the later spring ones would be.

She waved at her boss Alani through the window and kept going. Since it was Sunday and almost two o'clock, Alani would be closing soon. They kept short hours on Sunday so everyone who wanted to had a chance to go to church. She loved the Samashimas and how they treated all their workers like family, just as their parents before them had.

Fog hung like a damp blanket over the emerald rows that stretched back toward the foothills. The smell of damp earth and mulch enveloped her, causing her shoulders to ease down. As she headed past the main building where her office was, she noted all the lights were off. The Samashimas kept work minimal on Sundays, an aberration in this modern world. But they believed in the importance of rest, regardless of your religious beliefs, as part of the natural order of things, that working seven days a week would make you less productive, not more.

Cait wasn't so sure. She didn't work here on Sundays, but she couldn't remember the last Sunday she wasn't working on restoring her farmhouse, even when she sang in the choir at church for three services. But the house was another problem she was escaping today.

She declined an invitation to go out to lunch with other singles from church, sort of an anti-Valentine's Day thing. But she was at a frustrating point with her house renovation, and she needed a break.

It wasn't that she was anti-Valentine's Day; she had good memories of it with her Grandma. They'd always make a special dessert. When she was eleven, they'd made a strawberry soufflé. Her mouth watered even now thinking of it. She had considered making something today, but with no one to share it with, she'd be eating dessert all week.

She'd learned to enjoy her own company from years of eating microwave dinners in front of the TV while her parents were out. Once Grandma had taught her to cook, her meals improved. But cooking was always better when done for more than one person. Maybe she should have invited the singles over to her house. But with as much of it in shambles as it was, it probably wasn't safe.

And now she was thinking far too much for a day where she was supposed to escape with her camera.

Far enough into the fields, she stopped and looked around. The fog created lovely tendrils of mist. The diffused sun laid a lovely, soft light on the young strawberry plants. Cait composed the image in her mind before lifting her camera. She took some readings, refined her settings, and then began shooting. After a few shots, she checked the display on the back of her camera. Satisfied, she let her work absorb her, pushing aside, for now, everything else that threatened to consume her.

***

Grayson Kendall slid the creeper out from under the '66 Mustang, wiping his hands on a rag. "Try that, Dad."

Dad cranked the key and, after a bit of sputtering, the old girl turned over and began running like a champ.

Grayson leaned under the hood and made some adjustments before closing it. "I think that'll do it."

Dad climbed out of the car and grinned. "Glad you figured it out. Just in time for me to take your mother for a little Valentine's Day spin." He tapped the roof.

"It's a little foggy to head out to the beach." Grayson picked up tools and began returning them to their places. He was glad his folks were happy. Maybe that'd be him too. Someday.

"Ah, we have our places you know nothing of. We've had a few years' practice, you know." Dad picked up the last tool, placed it in the drawer and pushed it shut.

"I know. Go have a good time."

"We will. I appreciate your help, son." Dad paused. "You have any plans?"

Grayson didn't miss the significance of the pause. That was about as prying as Dad got. "Oh yeah. Pizza and a movie and my couch." The pizza sounded good, and he'd probably have a movie playing in the background, but he'd be working on a new land development proposal he was trying to pull together. He had to get moving on it before someone else grabbed it, but he never seemed to have time with his other work. His folks thought he worked too hard as it was, even though they didn't quite understand what a real estate attorney did all day.

He opened the door to the house before this conversation could go any further. "I'm giving Mom a hug goodbye, and then I'll be out of here." Before Mom could start in on him too.

***

Cait leaned back and stretched. She'd been in some awkward positions getting the shots she wanted. Luckily, there was no one out here to witness her contortions. She couldn't wait to upload her photos to her monitor and see how they looked. She glanced at her phone. Whoa! She'd been out here for hours, much longer than she'd thought. Well, time did that when she was absorbed with something she enjoyed. It happened often when she was working on a house project.

Her stomach growled. Time to eat anyway. She headed back.

An odd sound floated across the field. Fog could carry sound in weird ways, but this almost sounded like running water. But there was no running water anywhere out in the fields. Back in the day, there used to be irrigation ditches, but now everything was done through drip irrigation.

In the barn area, there were pumps and faucets, but there was no way she should be able to hear any water from there out here. Plus, being Sunday, no one would be in the barn.

She stopped. Footsteps?

Maybe she was hearing things. Nope. Definitely water.

She hopped over rows of plants and headed to the access road where she could make better time. Orienting toward the sound of the water, she picked up her pace, but the fog made it more difficult to discern the direction of the sound. Closer now, it was definitely water.

A shape moved in and out of the fog. Someone else was here. Mario? None of this made any sense.

The fog parted, and she spied the irrigation controls. Water was spewing out all over the ground. One of them must have broken. She reached for her phone.

A man darted from behind one of the storage sheds, looked right at her, and froze. Tall, blond, broad shoulders. If he had a plaid shirt, he would look like a lumberjack.

Barely thinking, she brought up her camera and snapped off a bunch of shots. No idea if the settings were right or if she'd get anything usable.

The man's face reddened, and he ran toward the parking lot.

Shaking, she lowered the camera and fumbled for her phone. She touched the screen at Mario's number and gave him a brief rundown. As she talked, she jogged toward the irrigation controls. Water flooded in every direction, creating a rapidly-enlarging pond drowning the nearby strawberry plants. Her shoes immediately soaked through. "It looks like the lines were ripped off and the valves opened. I can try to shut them off."

"Do what you can." Mario's voice came through the phone.

She looked closer at the pipes coming out of the ground. "Scratch that. I won't be able to shut them off. Everything's been smashed open."

Mario swore. "I'll be out there right away. I'll call Makoa on the way. You call the police."

Cait stared at the disconnected phone. The police? Her boss, yes, he should know, and she was glad Mario was calling him and she didn't have to. The severity of what she was looking at stunned her. Water lapped her ankles. If they couldn't get this under control, they stood to lose a good part of their strawberry crop before it even got off the ground.

Gingerly stepping out of the water, she headed back to her car. She'd call the police and wait there for them since there was nothing she could do to stop the flow of water. Her stomach churned.

Rounding the farm store, she saw her lonely car in the parking lot. But it looked odd. It sat lower than normal. And she hadn't left the windows down.

A sick feeling threatened to overwhelm her. Her tires had been slashed and her windows smashed out. Hands shaking, she dialed 911.

Meet Jennifer Vander Klipp

I make beauty from neglect, order from chaos. I like fixing messes!

Mom to two and stepmom to four, Jennifer navigates the teens while battling her daughter's juvenile arthritis, exploring the delights of her son's Asperger's, keeping gluten free, and, oh yeah, running her own creative project management business (editing, marketing, project management, graphic design) along the way.

A California native transplanted to the Midwest, her favorite thing is discovering with her husband how much there is to love about seasons, snow, and the delight that is Michigan.

She's a bestselling author of romantic suspense and historical romance. Get free chapters of her latest books at www.JenniferVanderKlipp.com

You can find her at:
www.JenniferVanderKlipp.com
Twitter: @jvklipp
Facebook: AuthorJenniferVanderKlipp
Instagram: jlvklipp
Pinterest: Jennifer Vander Klipp

Books by Jennifer:

Historical Romance
Be Mine
Coming Home
The Road Home

Romantic Suspense
Promise Me
Protective Custody

Contemporary Romance
The Inn at Cherry Blossom Lane

Made in the USA
Coppell, TX
30 January 2022

72653149R00050